LITTLE GIRL Against THE WALL

"You must do the things
you think you cannot do"
~ Eleanor Roosevelt

Quimby, Pickford & Cheshire Publishers
7915 South Emerson Avenue, Suite 324
Indianapolis, IN 46237

© 2009 by Quimby, Pickford & Cheshire Publishers.
All Rights Reserved. All permissions filed with publisher.
This book and all related artwork is a part of the collective body of work, Psalms of Fern, by Girard Tournesol.
Printed in the United States of America

Little Girl Against The Wall
First Edition, October 9, 2009
ISBN 13: 978-0-9822510-4-1   ISBN 10: 0-9822510-4-1
Library of Congress Cataloging-in-Publication Data
Library of Congress Control Number: 2009936921
Little Girl Against The Wall
\ Thrushart, Joanne Patricia

Volume discounts are available from Quimby, Pickford & Cheshire and the author, for counseling, outreach and promotional purposes. The author is available for public speaking engagements at no fee.

All accounts, facts and representations herein are based on the author's best recollection, notes, writings, and poetry over the years. All other characters expressed or implied are completely fictional and any similarity to individuals living or deceased are unintentional.

All un-cited quotations are those of the author.

∞ The paper used in this publication meets the minimum requirements of the American National Standards for Information Sciences—Permanence of Paper for Printed Library Materials, ANSI Z39.48-1992.

Cover Artwork:
Jessica Lynn Dunn, ***I Contemplate Her Genuflecting***, watercolor and ink, merged with Dreamstime image of red brick wall using Adobe Photoshop.

LITTLE GIRL Against THE WALL

By

Patricia Thrushart

First Edition

DEDICATION

FASHION THEM WINGS
(MEMORIES ARE STRUNG LIKE KNOTS)

Fashion them wings when you come upon
them—a lost and crying boy or a little girl
against a wall—
(Memories are strung like knots)
Fashion them wings to break their fall
and bring them close to joy.
***(Upon a worry string that fingers
tease and tickle)***
Not of wax, not broken, like those of Icarus,
Nor shall they soar too close to searing pain,
***(And as we travel knot-to-knot
back to the heart—)***
But fashion them wings of feather-white light
and loft them up on plumes of luck
***(We each will find a little girl against a wall,
or a lost and crying boy)***
So they may soar with grace
to brush the face of Love.
***(And from the wisdom of our Now—
we can, we will, and we do—)***

Comfort them.

TABLE OF CONTENTS

DEDICATION

Fashion Them Wings
(Memories are strung like Knots........V

INTRODUCTION....................X

FOREWORD....................XII

ACKNOWLEDGEMENTS...........XIX

LITTLE GIRL AGAINST THE WALL
POEMS

Do Thoughts of One.....................22
A Dark Moist Place........................23
Nimue..24
Little Girl Against the Wall..............25
What Lives on
When Lust Departs?........................26
Vampire Bliss....................................27
When We are One,
Together, Love.................................28
Who was the Last Neanderthal.........30
Pasiphaë, Passing............................31

TABLE OF CONTENTS CONTINUED

I Once Found
in this Vaulted Place..................................32
New Fern Muse...33
Nimue's Heart..34
Woman on
the Edge of Time.......................................35
Vessel..37
The Blood
and Sweat of Mithras................................39
Mitochondrial Eve.....................................40
2:30 a.m..41
Come Friend...42

THE BREAST OF MY SISTER
(PAGE 43)

The Breast of My Sister............................46
Michael of All Angels...............................47
Denouement..48
The Ghosts..49
Thunder in Manhattan...............................50

TABLE OF CONTENTS CONTINUED

COSTA RICA, SUMMER 2009
(PAGE 51)

Arenal	52
Arenal (translated)	53
Moon Over Tamarindo	54
Life is Lived	55
Michael Jackson RIP	56
Tocar a Muerto	57
The Carnage	58
Homeward	59
The Song of Time is a River	60
Reflection	61
The Pain of Waiting	63
Africa Enveloped Us	64
The Strength but not the Reason	65
O Swan	66
To Find All In	67
I Walked a Beaten Level Path	68
Surreal	70
Ergo	71
The First Egg	72

TABLE OF CONTENTS CONTINUED

I LOVE SIERRA CLUB TRIPS!
(PAGE 73)

Soft Rain Falling	74
The She King	76
Because Love Must Plan	78
Galileo's Daughters	79
I Come to this Denouement	81
Is it Peace	82
Lone Gull	83
A Garden Enclosed	84
Doubt Creeps	86
Druid Rock	87
Last Thought Before I Sleep	88
Here are Flowers of the Fields	89
The Victim	91
Inter-fused	92
To what chthonic spirit	93
Time has an arrow	94
The Picture	95
The Moon is Known Best	96
We Walked a Path of Memory	97

BOOK-END DEDICATION ... 99

ABOUT THE AUTHOR ... 100

INTRODUCTION

   My friend, you hold in your hands a small miracle.

   You need to first understand as you read my book that I had a fragile childhood.

   I have written poetry for years. But I never thought of myself as a poet. I wrote for one person—myself. I had no thought of sharing my writing even casually with my closest friends or my family, much less through the book you are holding now.

   I retreated to poetry—along with music, nature and books—as a little girl in this unhappy childhood. Poetry, pantheism, music, and literature—these were the pillars of my interior world and literally saved me from self-destruction.

   I spent a great deal of time in this interior place. As I experienced a home life infused with stress, and the uncaring and punitive environment of religious-affiliated grade schools, I shrank emotionally to the size of a mustard seed.

   In that tiny place where no one could join me, I wrote poetry, I sang, I played instruments; I walked in the woods and learned the songs of birds, or read about and imagined myself in the drawing rooms of 18th century England. Austen, Wordsworth, Thoreau, Emerson, Frost, and Yeats—I chose these voices to fill my head.

   This withdrawal protected me but did not heal me. The external person seemed strong, sure, and accomplished as she earned two college degrees, pursued a career that has led to a senior management position in a large money-center bank, earned a third-degree black-belt, became an accomplished semi-professional musician, and provided for the well-being of her two beautiful children.

But look further and the brokenness starts to show: two failed marriages, an inability to show the vulnerability necessary for friendship, a lack of self-acceptance…the little voice in my head always telling me "not good enough." Did I say earlier that I didn't think of myself as a poet? Let me be completely honest. I didn't even think of my writing as poetry. I called it parody. "Not good enough." This is why I call this book a small miracle.

Each of us thinks we own the indistinct memories of our past and the imagined promise of our future, but all we really have is Now. Today, as I write this, I love my family and rejoice in our intertwined care and support of each other. We are so lucky to have one another.

And Now, through some happy force (call it Luck, call it Agape Love, call it God) I find myself at a denouement that includes the great blessings of acceptance and forgiveness. In sharing my poetry I hope to share the promise of these blessings with you. If they came to me, they can come to you.

Within each of us is a little girl against a wall, or a lost and crying boy. As Buddha taught, the human condition at its very heart must include suffering. My story of pain may be different from yours, but in this we are the same: We are on a journey. We have suffered pain.

We CAN find acceptance.

FOREWORD

Welcome to my interior life. I invite you in with amazement and joy.

And, it must be said, some trepidation.

The exercise of writing this introduction—a requirement of my excellent publisher—has forced me to think tactically and analytically about an activity I do almost instinctively. And yet, I have come to several conclusions.

One is that my poetry arises from just one of two sources: intense emotional feelings or intellectual engagement. Perhaps this is yet another testimony to the theory of the right-brain, left-brain phenomenon explored by psychology and physiology.

I think both approaches are legitimate, and certainly both have precedent in the great sweep of poetic literature I have humbly and sincerely studied over the years. But I often find, after rereading the intellectually inspired poems I've written, they seem sterile. You'll be able to tell which is which—and I wonder which will resonate most with you and what that may tell you about yourself as a reader of poetry. The realization that I had a right-brain and a left-brain approach to writing poetry came to me after I wrote the poem "New Fern Muse" while fully participating in an important and fast-paced training session at work (my apologies to the facilitator).

In my notebook, on the left, were my comprehensive notes from the session. On the right-hand side of the page, I wrote the poem.

Simultaneously.

You may not believe me, but I sincerely

feel one did not detract from the other. This was a revelation to me, and I became more aware of my orientation from that point on. Sometimes I feel like two poets as a result.

That poem, incidentally, was meant to celebrate the journey of a friend who had successfully overcame great loss in his life and had turned his pain into healing and inspiration for others. It also established the Fern as a symbol for my Muse (as poets must have as Muse)—a symbol that you will find in many of my poems. I am a big fan of themes and enjoy finding commonalities between seemingly disparate concepts.

Actually, my Liberal Arts degree could also be called a four-year, expensive dally in comparative literature—with a few other disciplines thrown in for good measure and University requirements. So, naturally, I have chosen to muse about the poems in this book through a series of themes. As a woman of "middling age" and the mother of a teenage daughter, I have explored the themes of aging, beauty, and womanhood with more and more intensity.

It is interesting to find myself just barely approaching self-acceptance at the same time my daughter begins her journey of physical self-awareness. I ache to protect her from the mistakes and dead ends I pursued. "Pasiphaë Passing" explores the desire for perfection and its pursuit through cosmetic alteration. "Woman on the Edge of Time" tackles the struggle that I have had to accept my aging in a culture that worships the beauty of Youth. Oh, you too?

Join me, then, in the new celebration of women beautiful at any age. Can we really do that? YES!

"Nimue So Perfect a Name" raises the often-explored theme of compartmentalizing women into either whores or saints. I hope our daughters find these challenges less formidable than I did as our culture evolves a more human, balanced view of women. Let's lead this evolution, shall we? Let's start with our own daughters.

Speaking of daughters, some of my poems can be seen as exploring female Rites of Passage. "The First Egg" juxtaposes an imagined celebration of a girl's first menses by an ancient tribal matriarch and the embarrassment that surrounds this natural and beautiful moment today. I encourage every mother of a young daughter to celebrate her first flow in a special way. We must end this crazy view of menstruation as a burden or embarrassment! (Just recall every advertisement for feminine protection!)

I wrote "Vampire Bliss" after talking with my daughter about the Twilight series of books, and reading an extremely well written article in *The Atlantic Monthly* about their popularity.

The idea that hundreds of thousands of adolescent girls found a vampire to be their idea of the perfect boyfriend put me into a tailspin. If you were a fan, I apologize, but the whole thing upset me. I am still asking myself why.

Finally, in this theme, I include the title poem of this book, "Little Girl against The Wall." This was written after telling a very dear work friend about my childhood—something I rarely did before now. I tried to explore how to best deal with painful memories and how well I was dealing with my own, borrowing from a metaphor often used by one of my favorite authors, Anaïs Nin.

It will be obvious to any reader that this poet has been blessed with the experience of great love in my life; love that has been explored physically and emotionally; love that has brought to the fore many questions—and so beautifully, many answers—about self-acceptance, age, beauty, commitment and sexuality. The poems I have written to explore the love between a man and a woman (realized and expressed physically, emotionally and intellectually), and the great Agape Love of the Universe, are the most intense of any I have ever produced over decades of writing.

As an extremely reserved and private person, it has required a great courage of me to include them in this book. As you read these, monitor your own reaction. Recognition? Disbelief? Desire? Something else? That reaction may present to you an area of self-exploration to pursue. It certainly did that to me.

Relationships also have risks—and with these risks, fear and doubt. I explored these darker thoughts in poems like "Doubt Creeps," "What Remains," and "The Ghosts of Lovers Past." I have learned that it takes tremendous courage to surrender to true Agape Love, and these poems reflect my own struggle with disbelief and doubt. And friend, by no means is this battle won.

One reward of surrender can be self-acceptance; and it is only now, in my fifth decade of life, that I am poised to accept myself completely.

This is what I have called "Denouement," and I have written several poems that either celebrate that moment, or beg for it. There is only one place that such complete acceptances can occur—it is in the NOW of this moment. I invite you there through these poems.

One process I had to go through was to silence the little voice in my head that kept up, like an insidious Greek Chorus, an ongoing litany of undermining declarations. A very dear friend suggested I use the imagery of trapping that voice in a rock. I married this with the old Celtic belief that supernatural beings lived in trees, knolls and rocks—and wrote "Druid Rock."

Friends, this technique has worked. I have a boulder in my front garden where the voice lives, and I have written my poem on its face for good measure. And I am not crazy!

One barrier to self-acceptance and living in the Now is the fear of loss—whether due to death, the loss of a lover to another, or the perceived deterioration of beauty through aging. Friends dear to me have lost loved ones and have struggled with intense grief as a result. Others have lost lovers or jobs.

Several poems in this book explore loss; my most treasured is "Flowers of the Fields" written beside the grave of a dear man who was father to a dearer son.

At his grave I confronted my own fears of loss and found that peace was there. We all have this innate ability to overcome great loss in our lives and eventually even celebrate the "letting go" we all must do.

If you are holding on to some grief or loss, I hope you find the great relief and peace that forgiveness or letting go can bring.

My sister was recently diagnosed with breast cancer, and in that moment, my family and I joined the millions of women and their families fighting this disease and facing a poignantly more real sense of mortality. I turned to poetry for self-expression and wrote "The Breast of My Sister." You'll find an essay on this topic later in the book.

When Michael Jackson died, I was staying at a Bed & Breakfast in Costa Rica with other Americans, and we discussed his life. I felt great empathy for him and realized he was another lost and crying boy. My poem on his death probably does not do this empathy justice.

Lastly, my friend, you'll find some poems that I wrote to capture my simple intellectual curiosity over a concept.

These poems were usually the result of reading an article or book in my usual areas of interest—the origins of the universe, the history of humankind, the mysteries of physics, or the workings of the human brain. Poems such as "One," "The Song of Time," and "Time Inferred," introduce you to the topics rattling around in my head when left to my own devices.

I hope the eclectic mix of poetry you find here will be a starting point for a long conversation between us, and one that helps me speak to you in the future about more specific topics and themes should we have this privilege again.

I hope so.

You now know more about what is going on in my head than most of the people around me. In reading this book you enter my heart, my mind, and my thoughts as intimately as my closest friend. If nothing else, may it spark in you a desire to know, and then accept yourself, NOW—in this moment. Read on.

ACKNOWLEDGEMENTS

Every writer has a host of people to thank—for without the support, love, and shared experiences that friends and family offer, few writers have much to share. My love for my parents and sisters cannot be overstated—we have been through the journey together and have reached a caring place we are fortunate to find. To my daughter—that I could have someone so beautiful, perceptive and talented in my life brings me much joy and wonder. To my son—I have learned much from your introspection, ethical musings and creative expression. Your talent and sensitivity are great treasures. I am blessed to have you both so close to me. To my godmother—you were the first to accept me without equivocation for who I am. You may not even realize what that has meant to me. To the friends who work with me, who sing with me, who pursue that next belt in karate with me, thank you for your support and encouragement. To my publisher—thank you for convincing me that my poetry was just that. Your work to bring this book into being is a great gift to me. Kathy Carlson's objective and thorough editorial review made this book exponentially better. Thanks to Jessica Lynn Dunn for her amazing art work. And finally, to my Fern Muse—whose psalms lined my path toward healing and self-acceptance—thank you. Your support and friendship are blessings beyond measure.

"Courage is the price
that life exacts for
granting peace"

~ Amelia Earhart

LITTLE GIRL AGAINST THE WALL

POEMS

Do Thoughts of One

Do thoughts of one
rule out the others—
sisters—daughters—
mothers—
brothers—are these
overwhelmed
surrendered
by constant thoughts of
an agape
lover?
NO—
FOR as space balloons
from 10^{-36} to NOW,
a stretching fabric
of everything
bringing with it—relentlessly—
whole galaxies—worlds—
the fiercest black holes—whorled—
dark energy—intractably—
anti-matter—helplessly—
moving outward—inexorably—
SO TOO
Love expands—exponentially—
to effortlessly embrace
ALL

A Dark Moist Place
(or fetal dreaming)

A dark moist place
cushioned
warm—
alive through chord-brought
blood—and
flood
of protein—
asleep from placental
adenosine—
and as he sleeps
of what would he dream?
Before the sight of green or flesh
before the sound of voice enmeshed
before the memory of the day
of what would he dream?
of primal life in egg
or zygote?
Heaven's gate
or lives once lived?
Muffled cries of sibling waiting—
or the last late look at the
mindful face
of God?
Of what would he dream?

NIMUE

Such power the sages split you in two.
Enfleshing the evil seductress—to fear—
Firmly submerging the rest—never near—
beneath a placid surface.
Divided, diminished, now easily vanquished,
to fit the non-druid dominion of men.
But you are yet both and yet all, Nimue—
Keeping hereafter the warrior's sword,
Trapping forever the sorcerer's heart.
Fierce magic growing—
Cave waiting—
Lake moving—
And look! A sword thrusts through
the shimmering shroud!
Nimue waking, Nimue shining,
Nimue perfectly rising,
as One.

Little Girl Against the Wall

Little girl against the wall
Were you a victim of it all
Or are you the Minotaur
Stalking through my weedy past—
Labyrinth of a thousand vast
dead ends and darkling corners?
Is that trembling or are you
crouched to strike like memories do?
Am I Pasiphaë—nurse—
Or Theseus—final curse—
Do I comfort you
or slay you?

What Lives on When Lust Departs?

What lives on when lust departs?
What keeps the heart
Engaged
When sinews slacken
in each part that makes the body rise?
Rush of hormones fickle—
androgen and estrogen—
trickle.

What lives on when lust departs?
What keeps the parts
Entwined
When cells sicken—
body thickened.
Oxytocin, vasopressin,
Right ventricle tegmental attraction.

Attachment.

Vampire Bliss
(Daughters of a Thousand Dreams)

Daughters of a thousand dreams
Schemers of a thousand schemes
of beauty, romance, passion.
Lusting for a vampire's kiss
(His restraint creates your bliss
if only you could know it).
The rhythmic moon now in your blood,
emotions streaming like a flood
behind a sweet complexion.
Lift the book before your eyes.
Live the menace that we try
to shield you from completely.
Twilight of a child's view—
rapture mixed with fear—on cue—
beneath your budding bosoms.
A Boy-man who would love so much
he cannot bring himself to touch
lest his strange violence hurt you.
Ravage me, you implore
from the safety of the floor
in your young sacred bedrooms—
Desire that which rips apart,
the innocence once at the heart
of Girl-ness.

When We are One Together, Love

When we are one together, love,
what travels will we take
What pilgrimage will call us forth
from bed and book and plate
Will we return to former haunts
to exorcise our pasts
(Jamaica—land of coffee trysts,
the sand a fine caress
Paris—place of lovers' strolls
and bones so long at rest)
When we arrive and place our feet
on paths once walked before
who will step out to greet us—
who will be at the door
of this new memory
(a former lover or an unknown host?)
and as our arms entwine
and as we walk our rhythm new
will we push past the sadness
of the loves that were not true
Do places of our past exist
outside our knits of time
can they be fast reclaimed
and earn a place in our new clime
of gentle words and tumbled cotton sheets
where trust is harbored strong
or are they blemished, torn and smeared
by memories forlorn
And as we wile hours on the beach—
Champs Elysees—

CANTO CONTINUED

Will we become a marker
to a couple on their way
to their own future
as we are to our pasts—
travelers in space and time
with wisdom at the last:
Oh yes—and as we visit them—
our former selves and broken vows—
we smile, wave, and bless them
from this moment we call NOW.

Who was the Last Neanderthal
(Those Thousands Years Ago)

The last
One
The Very Last
One
An Elder
Keeper of the Fire
Without the need to light
One
A baby crying in a cave with no
One
Left to feed her
A man of muscle and scar with no
One
Left to mate
A woman fertile and engorged with no
One
Left to suckle
A boy without
One
Tool to hunt
A girl without
One
Will to eat
Who was the last
One
The Very Last
One

Pasiphaë, Passing

Pasiphaë, passing,
fair
the smell of grass is in her hair,
straining toward the shining bull—
the object of desire

Desperate beauty,
soft caress,
moonlike skin and flowing dress—
leaning on his sweaty flank,
all absent of desire

Artificer
Daedalus,
fashion her to spark his lust,
stretching hide across a form
creating his desire

(Where she is thick—thin
Where she is soft—hard
Where she has less—more
Where she is old—new)

Pasiphaë,
womb engorged,
lust relieved
by seed outpoured,
birthing into life a curse—
the monster of desire

I Once Found in this Vaulted Place

I once found in this vaulted place
A comfort in its mindless grace
People joined in dance and sin—
a Gentle Time
when chanted consonants swept like wind.

Now lifted face and cupped hands,
tearful glance from stalwart man,
every hymn I ever heard—
they baffle me
Since faith flew, like a startled bird.

New Fern Muse

Spring fern
unfurling
My Poet long lost
among the nodding poppies
of Duty, Details, Drive.
Fresh-fiddle-green
resolute—
rising from past detritus,
singing psalms
of healing—
of beauty beyond pain.
Emerging, brave,
in the dappled-sun
clearing
of mind and memory.
Deep roots sustain
chlorophylled fronds.
Perennial Survivor.
Now drenched in rain tears
Now tossed by winds
Now food for buck and doe.
Soft, muse, soft and see—
your songs float as spores
across the crystal stream.

Nimue's Heart

Nimue's Heart,
pain-forged
steel-girded
safely ensconced in a bone-laced cage.
Husbanded,
docile,
domestic and tranquil,
carefully beating to middling age.

A spear, out of nowhere!
A parry! A thrust!
Pierced to the seed!
Pierced—with a rush
of frisson and fire—
like Sybyl's before—
blue-red veins throbbing,
hands trembling,
sword falling,
received with a ripple into the deep.
The new non-wound pulsing,
a throbbing, a longing,
a magnified beating
of Nimue's Heart.

Woman on the Edge of Time

Woman on the edge of time,
Unflinching—you deserve
Grace to age as Age departs
a grace to every earthly turn.

Wrinkles not the stuff of shame
of scalpel or of cream—
badges of an act-filled life
lived full and wide and deep.

Gravity a force—not foe—
a source of centeredness.
Scars the map of sacrifice
to child, fate or dare.

Not toward you the loud speech used
with strangers or the slow.
Reverence—for the wisdom
in your step, and hand, and brow.

Reverence for the life poured out
from vessel shaped by fire—
Reverence for the brittle strength—
each bone, each glance, each breath.

Past the mindless worship
of blind Youth's fertility
where sex and pheromone propel
each feeling, choice and deed.

CANTO CONTINUED

Not by tricking time do you
earn praise or poetry
Not for pity, nor for shame
do others hold you dear.

Woman on the edge of time
poised with Eternity
heart and mind now shining
in their great translucency.

Vessel

Vessel—
the stuff of stars
formed.
Smooth
Perfect
from the potter-mother's womb.
Love pours in
its sacred oil
but
Fate
Delivers
Blows.
Jarred—then
Cracked—then
Broken.
But not quite empty.
Seeking—
to fill up,
to feel "up,"
to heal up.
Open.
Accepting any fluid to be full.
With each forced drop—cracks widen.
Crumbling.
But then
a hand
of knowing
a hand
of tenderness
a hand
of kindness
Touches

CANTO CONTINUED

clay
Touches
vessel
and
Heals
Forever.

The Blood and Sweat of Mithras

The blood and sweat of Mithras
is mixed upon his chest
struggling with sacrifice—
testosterone's behest.
Straddling the heavy flanks,
a hand pulls back the horns.
Below the arch-ed neck
the weapon glints steel-born.
Bellowing, the bull protests
the scent of death—its fear
matched in force unyielding
by the man that holds it near.
A slice of knife, the spill of blood—
is the conquest done?
Strong enough? Big enough?
Manhood must be won
struggling with the demons
crowding male expectancy—
how long? and for how long—
performance soon to be
judged by little handshakes
judged by women's eyes
judged by myth and legend
Mithras chokes, and dies.

Mitochondrial Eve

Imagine her tall—
wide-hipped,
full-lipped,
broad feet splayed
on clay-earth-Africa.

Imagine her strong—
brown-skinned,
un-sinned,
round breasts filled
with mother-sweet-milk.

Imagine her then—
sister-strong,
men gone,
protecting the children
of new-sapiens-tribe.

Imagine her now.

Across the spangled expanse of human time
through drought-death,
famine-despair,
through failed hunts,
desperate migration,
through man-war
Her Children Survive.
Only Hers.

2:30 A.M.

2:30 a.m.
A voice begins—
tense chant—
driving, striving
mocking-bird:
"It IS true," "It IS true," "It IS true"
flowing
"My point," "My point," "My point"
ringing the wet streets
filling pavement cracks
streaming through windows
"I AM right," "I AM right," "I AM right"
rising
constant
louder
insistent
assaulting sleep
assaulting ears
assaulting breath
to a crescendo of tears.
Buried
another voice joins
blurry, low
indistinct
mourning dove
no, no
no
no
no

Come Friend

Come friend
and we will walk
across the small flat black disc
of my conscious mind
which floats in the expanse
of not-knowing.
We will walk as far as we can
and then
stand in each others arms
on the trembling edge.
We will fall
and—
will we fall   together?
will we fall   apart?

THE BREAST OF MY SISTER

I cried when my sister called to tell me her mammogram was suspicious. But I couldn't let her hear me. I had to be strong, the oldest sister, the surrogate mom. I soothed her: "I had a 'call-back' after a mammogram, too. It was just a calcification—nothing serious. I am sure it is nothing." But I knew that there was in fact "nothing" I could say that would lift the fear that choked her. She faced a waiting game—an appointment, another picture, and a diagnosis. In time, these came to pass—and unlike my experience, her diagnosis was all she feared. She has cancer.

To women of our age, the word is a death-knell. We grew up when it was the great incurable disease synonymous with death. In fear, panic and desperation she begged me—"take care of my girls for me."

And what of our girls? My daughter, her daughters, my nieces, my sisters? Instantaneously we went from ordinary to "high-risk" because of the breast of my sister. Life has changed not just for her, but also for us, and for our granddaughters and grandnieces yet unborn. We all now have the matriarchal curse of a close relative with breast cancer.

I promised my sister three things—that I would love her girls like my own always, and that I would walk with her, next May, in the Race for the Cure. I promised her that this would not kill her.

And it won't.

My sister is lucky among those who face this—she caught it early, small, contained, and curable. She will not lose her hair, she will not lose her strength, she will not lose her breast—she has lost only the blissful ability to ignore her patent mortality. All of us lost this—with her. With two incisions, she will live as all of us will live now, a little more aware of death, and concurrently more grateful of the gift every day of life brings.

And may I say this to every woman: **Get your yearly mammogram. Practice self-examination. Choose awareness. Be a survivor.** This is the most important message. It was only through her routine observation of yet another appointment that my sister saved her own life. SAVED HER OWN LIFE.

And join us, please, in the Race for the Cure, and any other event or fundraiser that insists this insidious disease be cured. For you, for your daughters or daughters-in-law, for your granddaughters, for your friends. The root causes of this attack on the part of our bodies designed to sustain life must be understood! Hormonal? Environmental? Related to lifestyle? All of the above? We must know and demand a "cure"—and ever-improving medical treatment. Who will advocate for this most womanly of diseases if not us?

I wrote "The Breast of My Sister" in response to this traumatic moment in the life of my family and any family that soldiers through this diagnosis with one of its own. In part, I wanted the poem to celebrate the breast as the source of mother-sweet-milk, an ancient symbol of fertility and of womanliness—beautiful to anyone of any age and gender. In this way I hoped to make the cancer seem even more obscene, like the Worm in Blake's Rose. "Oh rose thou art sick." It is a sickness we can cure if, caught early enough. And it is a sickness that ultimately we must learn to prevent.

(At the time of publication a second sister had just received the news that her mammogram was initially suspicious, but it was thankfully benign after we painfully waited for the biopsy report. The sister who inspired this poem needed chemotherapy after all; we have sat with her through the struggle and have great hope in her excellent prognosis. She will be deemed cancer free soon. My mammogram was normal this time around and so was my mother's. The last of my three sisters has yet to get hers, and, I am gently reminding her to do so.)

The Breast of My Sister

The breast of my sister
nourished her young
inflamed her lovers
pleasured her nights.
Glands of sweet milk
sung by the poets,
painted by artists
rosy and white.
Cuneiform symbol
captured in marble,
sculpted in clay
for fertility rites.
Firm fiber tissue
harbors a secret
hardened and evil—
a cancerous blight.
Hormonal? Genetic?
Poison? Or Fate?
The struggle for life,
the strength for the fight—
god willing, love hoping,
(oh sweet god-love willing)
is growing to gird her
growing to shield her
is growing with might
in the breast of my sister.

Michael of All Angels

Michael of all angels—
Creator—like the God
massaging life from rib and clay—
stones cry out as you tread
through quarry beds of starry dust.
Marble-veined pulses throb as you pass—
to be felt, to be flaked,
to be smoothed, to be struck,
to be lovingly let out.
For seven days of seven years,
your breath upon the rock,
your sweat upon the slab—
under your hand contours congeal:
Draped.
Cold.
Obdurate.
Apart.
Lidded.
Languid.
Frozen
Pain—
Pieta.

Denouement

We will need mercy sweet, my love
when all is said and done.
Portia's rain from heaven
on the hearts that others shunned.
For knots tied up in crimps of pain
Denouement awaits,
resolution's gift of Hope
from Love—arriving Late.
Love—that pulls at old threads
stuck in intricate design-
vows and duty woven through
the fabric used to bind
our future up-the past a cloak
of habit and demand—
But each string of occurrence taut
led up to where we stand
Now. A new-worked tapestry
of peace with who we are—
acceptance of each nub and fray
the weaver left un-darned.
De-knotted, raveled threads unwind
the fear that reason holds—
Denouement awaits, my weft,
its mercy fine, but bold.

The Ghosts

The Ghosts
of Lovers past
Breathe cold
upon the Heart.
Once fond icy fingers
fondle dendrites frozen
in half-memories
and full regrets.
Rasped whispers,
rusted lust,
oxidized chains
Rattling Now.
Doubt is their haunt.
Trust is their prey.
Certainty—their price.

Thunder in Manhattan

Early one morning I heard her—
Her buildings shrouded in gray guilt,
Her rattling breath drawing paper
down empty avenues—
A city swelled with a horde
of strangers, deflated.

With a fatigue of decades—
the memories of raging fire,
the tramp of millions seeking
sudden freedom,
bleary, dreary, smeary hellos,
cruel goodbyes,
From the ache of hating them all
and needing them all—
She groaned.

COSTA RICA, SUMMER 2009

As we drove away from Volcan Arenal, which was completely cloud-covered the entire time we were there, the wind began to persistently blow away the clouds—roiling up her sides revealing her lava fields. We never saw the caldera, but my sister was finally able to see that there was, in fact, a volcano there. I was so happy for her; she wanted to see it so badly! For two days you would have never known there was anything there.

So here is my poem; of course, it is a poem of love and seduction.

Arenal

Montaña oculta—
Imperturable.
Las nubes tu enagua fruncida,
Las cenizas tu piel seca.
Timida dormilon.
El fuego de tus entrañas—
Latente.
Pero—ah—
subito—
te siente un amante,
el viento!
Suavisisimo, insistente sus caricias!
Eleva tu refago—
el besa tus flancos cenizos.
Y de abajo su tacto—
Esmeralda!
Y interior—
te encendes!
Y tu corazón—
se brilla!

Arenal
(TRANSLATED)

Concealed mountain
imperturbable
the clouds your frilly petticoat
the ash your dry skin
shy sleepyhead
the fire of your innermost place
latent
but—ah—suddenly
you feel a lover, the wind!
so soft, insistent his caresses!
he lifts your slip
he kisses your ash-colored flanks.
and under his touch—emerald.
and inside—you kindle!
and your heart glitters!

Moon Over Tamarindo

Heavy she lies
and languid
above the restless palms
full with round fecundity
succor of the night

luxuriant and glowing
in golden stolen light
preening in her passage
through clouds of silken white

beneath her heavy body
the sea stirs and responds
earth's bulging rock strains upward
desirous and blind

Life is Lived

Life is lived
Now.
A Mandala of choices
with spokes of kindness
Encased
in a circled rim
of Friends
Revolving
endlessly
around a centered hub
of evolving Love.
Turning from brokenness
Turning from hurt
Each gyration reunifying the
Self
with the
Cosmos.

Michael Jackson RIP

Bleached face
Lips traced
Mirrored eyes
And scarring.
Moonwalk
Glottal stops
Skeleton
Goes dancing
Children kept
Never slept
Pills to mask
The aching.
Tragic clown
Lowered down
In a grave now hidden.

Tocar a Muerto

To play a death
Upon a bell
To dance among the gravestones
To sing a dirge
Of derry-down
Among the flocking ravens.
To grieve a loss
To lose a life
Of promise and of meaning.
To mean the truth
To truth a lie
To lie
Among the living.

The Carnage

The carnage of
An evening light
Lies littered on
The tiled floor—
Singed silver
Gossamer wings,
blackened blue
Iridescent thoraxes,
Curled feathered
Unfeeling antennae
Battered from
The desperate flights
To fuse their fine
Soft bodies with
a faux Neutron star which,
Burning
Constant—but unfaithful,
Hot—but dispassionate,
Bright—but unthinking,
Illuminates their
Funeral pyre spiral
To the floor.

Homeward

Join me in
the love I feel
with daughter's head
all in my lap
relaxed and trusting
as she naps
her hair spread out like lace.

Join me in
the love I feel
with son's soft eyes
now meeting mine
to tell me of a Buddhist line
his mala bracelet twisting.

Join me in
the love I wish—
a future full of times
like this—
a family blended
in its strength
of caring and connection.

The Song of Time is a River

The Song of Time is a river,
the one that seems to flow—
the one we try to understand
through Causality.
A river both unchanging,
yet changing constantly—
its fluid path mapped in the mind,
remembered differently each time.
Heraclitus first posed it—
a sublime Paradox:
Into the same River
we do
and do not
step.

Reflection
(Cluny Tapestry)

Her hands lie folded in her lap,
She sits in meadowsweet and rue,
crimp and crinoline her dress,
a signet on her finger.

Flaxen braids outline her brow,
no wrinkle or adornment there.
Steady eyes regard the world
of castle and refinement.

She waits, a mirror in her hand,
the glass of revelation rests.
No interest in her own visage—
modesty becomes her.

And shy, a unicorn appears
drawn to the contemplation there—
hesitates across the moor
as if to sense intention.

And soft, she lifts the mirror up
and turns the sliver toward him.
Waves of light capture his face—
the horn a spiraled scepter.

Drawn to it as a babe to milk
he prances to her skirted side,
draws his delicate legs up
and nestles at her bosom.

CANTO CONTINUED

The joy of gazing at the face
of such unbridled beauty wild
replaces loneliness long felt—
there is not one, but two now

The Pain of Waiting

The pain of waiting
for one
Word
of Status
or of
Solace
will stretch an Hour
Singular
into an Abyss
Infinite.
Within that fearful rending
Place
of frantic heart
and spinning mind
a great and ponderous
Truth
 is found:
Love
is at once
a burden
and a
Joy.
Terrible.
Ineffable.
and
Real.

Africa Enveloped Us

Africa enveloped us
its warm and sandy walls—
the bed a living cradle—
the chipping sparrow's call
our morning serenade
to do what we will do
in battle hollow
living full
a stream of love
a hill of joy
a view of future bliss—
Africa afforded this.

Signed:
Patricia Thrushart
Plantation Bed and Breakfast
Africa Room Guest Log

The Strength
but not the Reason

The Strength—but not the Reason
The Light—but not the Truth
The Foil—not the Action
The Shield—but not the Fall.

The Mirror—not the Image
The Bandage—not the Wound
The Crutch—but not the Bone
The Clock—but not the Pace.

The Way—but not the Journey
The Hope—but not Belief
The Dream—but not the Waking
The Goal—but not the Path

O Swan

O Swan
You were a man
In making you
Divine
They rob you of your greatness—
GRAVE ROBBERS
of an entombed memory—
Because
What you did, any god could do
dozing away centuries
in a hot afternoon's nap,
Christianity a humid, fitful dream.

But you, great one, had a
Man's
limitations and still
(I know them well, I've slept with them)
you
SPOKE.
And breathed wisdom's life into
Time
Clocked in hours and days
Pivoting
on your BIRTH:
one man,
one life,
one great Love.

To Find All In

To find All In
is a
Gift of Time
a reckoning—
a beckoning—
like incense
rising plumes

To be All In
is a
State of Mind
A discipline—
like shaolin—
or ohm
forever sighed

To stay All In
is an
Act of Will
A certain Skill—
like focusing
on Zen-forgotten
koans

To lose All In
is a
Rift of Love
A dreary knell—
a lonely bell—
like Taps
across a stone

All In

I Walked a Beaten Level Path

I walked a beaten level path
of Solitude
and Surety.
It had some Beauty,
side-to-side
in Calmness
and Tranquility.
Ahead the way meant loneliness.
Behind lay all regret.
Above, the winds of Courage
rustled questions left
unsaid.
And as I walked the well-worn way
I came upon a Split.
A rough and rolling narrow thing—
verdant and unlit.
Ferns crowded at the entrance,
their fronds green shimmering
and deep within the gloom
I heard a bird call echoing.
Courage blew hard at my back,
but fear and habit stayed me.
I tried to pass—I could not move—
and Time sped forth to test me.
Which should I choose?
How can I turn?
Whom will I harm?
When will I learn
the Truth of every Action—
The Risk of any Choice—

CANTO CONTINUED

The Hope of a new Journey—
The Promise of each Path.
And this I realized,
as the winds of Courage bid me turn:
Life is for the living
and Risk lives in each step.

SURREAL

SURREAL
Becomes Real
Surpassing
Surrealistic
Notions
SURMOUNTING
Surface
Inclinations
Surrendering
Surprise
Inflections
Surrounding
Surplus
~~Fascinations~~
Surreptitiously
InSURing

SURVIVAL

ERGO

The link of thought and breath to self—
the tie of love to thought—
the weld of self to someone else—
the bond of hope to trust.
To Err no more
To Go the way
To Cogitate
the Sum of All.

Cogito ergo sum
Amo ergo cogito
Amo te
Ergo
Sum

The First Egg

The first egg
the first flow
the red rush
the moon's glow
a young girl
her hair long
her breasts high and firm.
The desert tribal
matriarch
mixes blood with earthen clay—
marks the daughter's head to show
that she's a woman now.
Her hair is tied in braid and reeds
a sash around her waist
a rite-full passage is observed
with joy in tents of grace.

The first egg
the first flow
the red rush
the moon's glow
a young girl
her hair short
liner-heavy eyes
a sterile kit
from Health class
a pad to mask the odor
embarrassed laugh
a closed door
a moment gone forever.

I LOVE SIERRA CLUB TRIPS!

One year the kids and I went with the Sierra Club to camp in Canyon de Chelly with the Navajo. Our first night we camped at the foot of Spider Rock. The Navajo believe that Spider Woman lives on top of the rock—it is She who taught the Navajo how to weave rugs, and who played an important part in their creation myths. Water and rain are sacred and spiritual as well. A soft misty rain is often called a Navajo rain.

We camped in the canyon for a week. Every morning, we'd hear canyon wrens and every night coyote calls echoing off the walls. Our guide—Daniel—would play a native flute against the wall to wake us. Wild horses ran through the arroyos. Daniel and his kin showed us sand painting and sang sacred songs around the nightly campfire.

When we climbed out of the canyon (at 7,200 ft above sea level, the canyon walls are 2,000 feet up—it was arduous for me) I saw an old man and woman, driving goats ahead of them, scampering up the canyon path as if it were flat. They had knapsacks on their backs. I was so humbled.

It was an incredible experience.

Soft Rain Falling

Soft rain falling
female rain
rain of crop
rain of clean
rinsing hogan, rug and dream
soft rain falling
soft rain

soft tears falling
female tears
tears of story
tears of joy
canyon glyphs and child's toy
soft tears falling
soft tears

soft rain falling
female rain
soft

soft rain falling
female rain
rain of crop
rain of clean
rinsing hogan, rug and dream
soft rain falling
soft rain

soft tears falling
female tears
tears of story
tears of joy

CANTO CONTINUED

canyon glyph and child's toy
soft tears falling
soft tears

soft years passing
female years
years of birthing
years of change
wrinkled face
and jointed pain
soft years passing
soft years
soft

The She King

(Hatshepsut 1479-1458 BC)

Hatshepsut
you would be "king"
a lion's mane
the cobra slain
a beard of wax
beneath the pharaoh headdress

(Fashion her better than all gods, shape for me
this my daughter, whom I have begotten)

Hatshepsut
your rounded chin
your breasts bound up
you drink the cup
of grape and myrrh
among your priests and nurses

(Her form shall be more exalted than the gods)

Hatshepsut
a man portrayed
a woman still
your heart is filled
with lapwing's song
with flutter for your Egypt

(Now my heart turns this way and that, as I think
what the people will say.

CANTO CONTINUED

Those who see my monuments in years to come,
and who shall speak of what I have done)

Hatshepsut
of Amun god
once buried plain
you built a reign
of obelisk
from Sinai to Nubia

(To look on her was more beautiful than
anything)

Because Love Must Plan

Because love must plan
I scour
my calendar for
hours
for days and nights and
flights
to mine those precious times of
ours
those moments certain
natural
when sleep becomes a dance
when time becomes a gift
when food becomes a tease
when wine becomes our breath
when music is our score
and
Love
Comes
Home

Galileo's Daughters

(The activities of the moons of Jupiter on August 18, 2009)

Galileo's daughters
dance attendance
on their god
Jupiter—
His body splayed
For pleasure and caress

His harem moons prepare
To do his will and his desire—
Tugged and teased
By his great mass
and by his banded strength

(he beckons them)

Io—shy—approaches
With her shadow in her wake
Trailing just to kiss
the barest edges of his limb

Europa lingers lovingly
Across his roiling face
To please him as he wishes
With her young and icy skin

Ganymede moves languid
To the great and growing spot
Red-infused
And throbbing

CANTO CONTINUED

As Europa fades
All spent

And Callisto stays away
At the furthest point she can
Far and fierce and
Jealous until
He calls to her again

And at that moment
he commands they give their love and strength
they fall together to create
a single glorious
pulsing
point of light

I Come to this Denouement

I come to this denouement
Imperfect, scarred and flawed—
but awed—
rejoicing in each striation
each thrombosis
vindication
but harshly holding over myself
impossible expectations
how can I be so unkind?
how can I still expect to find
inhuman self-perfection?
why do I think it even needed?
why would I think to even feed it
anything but love?

Is it Peace

Is it peace
that is sought
to be bought
through acreage
or books
is it peace
wanted from haunted
or daunted lives

It IS peace

Then what of risk?
The thrill of threat,
the threat of discovery,
the discovery of fear,
the fear of exposure,
the exposure of gambles,
Is there peace in peril
amity in danger
unanimity in liability?

is it peace
is it risk
is it both

IT IS

Lone Gull

Lone gull
one gray gull
blue dark flight
dull deep river
steel scraped sky
sheet brown rain
driving wind
one gray gull   winging

A Garden Enclosed

A garden enclosed
Our private life is precious
a sheltered hidden joy
a garden closed and savored
behind walls built thick and staid
ivy-grown and mossy
and almost passed unseen
but for the glow that spills
through crackles and keyholes
sacred and protected
from judging scrutiny
the pomegranate and the fig
give luscious fragrant meat
spikes of mullein rise
among many buttercups
bees a-dust with nectar
sting lips of orchid flowers
there, fantasy's a reveler
and playfulness the dew
a garden made more precious
shared by only two

(A garden enclosed is my sister, my spouse;
a spring shut up, a fountain sealed.
Thy plants are an orchard of pomegranates,
with pleasant fruits; camphire, with spikenard,
Spikenard and saffron; calamus and cinnamon,
with all trees of frankincense; myrrh and aloes,
with all the chief spices: a fountain of gardens,
a well of living waters, and streams from
Lebanon.)

CANTO CONTINUED

Awake, O north wind; and come, thou south;
blow upon my garden, that the spices thereof
may flow out.
Let my beloved come into his garden, and eat his
pleasant fruits.)

Doubt Creeps

Doubt creeps
crawls
falls
in cracks of Apart
insidious
hideous
cold
takes hold
made brave by
distance—
time and space—
no face
to face
Doubt creeps
crawls
creates walls

Druid Rock

The druid rock
traps evil speak
by streams that weep
and trees that moan
an ancient dirge—
knolls that whisper
bone cold tales—
cairns that call to
rusted blades
a voice is trapped
in silicate
hissing
insisting
to be freed
to wreck
to reap
to ring the wild bell
above the high
and windy night
to raise doubt
to frenzy fear
DON'T LET IT OUT
don't let it speak
the voice now trapped
in druid rock
by streams that weep
by trees that moan
keep it tricked
trapped
forever

Last Thought Before I Sleep

Last thought before I sleep
first thought as I arise
Now felt in sinew and bone
when alone—
in organ and gland
when I stand
with you
or lie
beside you
in sheets of sweetest mercy
under pillows of desire
and every neuron
every nerve
fervently
curved
around thoughts amazed
fire feverishly
to ask
WHAT IS THIS
This?

Flowers of the Fields

Here are flowers of the fields
Gathered in your name
Michael
The brush of a thrush's wing
The sound of a harp string
As if angels sing
From the future you dreamt
Where you are loved
In constancy
As a vireo sings above
Your grave—
Incessantly—
Hidden from view
Like you
But present still
(Be it your will)
Revealed in story
Missed in song
Re-called in poem
Mourned in tears
We face our fears of loss
Michael
Perhaps of a lover
to another
Or pain of death
or loss of breath
Through mold
In folds of lungs
The loss of tongue
The fear of age

CANTO CONTINUED

Or loss of wage
And through all this
The vireo chants our fate
And you await
Michael
And you await

(In paradisum deducant te angeli
in tuo adventu suscipiant te martyres)

The Victim

The victim
of a lightening strike
flung hard and through the air and
shot with streamers blue and fierce
and pressure pulsing force
will find
should she survive this special time
and keep her heart from fainting
that fern-like burns
have marked her skin—
aborescent
erythema—
as if the surging charge
had traced
the sweet songlines of sweat.
Marked so by Fern,
Struck so by Force,
in lapiz laser light
she ends up asking How—
and What—
since afterwards her heart
will skip
in luminescent
effervescent
glorious
arrhythmia.

(Apologies to Gretchen Ehrlich and "A Match To The Heart")

Inter-fused

Inter-fused
by Agape—
Volutional and
Active.
No conditions—unconditioning.
Sacrificial—sacred.
past Storge, Eros, Philia—
Organic and original.
Apodictic:
Essential
Nature of
Love itself—
Divine.

To what chthonic spirit

To what chthonic spirit
owe I tithe or gratitude—
burnt offering—
blood suffering—
for loneliness once wooed.
What deity from underground
will rise up to defend
heart rituals—
soul victuals—
which no longer mend
past chaotic thoughts
of doubt and vicissitude—
or guilt of what's deserved,
or how the past is viewed.
Call up the Pantheon—
who stands to fight the fight?
a little boy at play in air
above a goddess standing fair.

TIME HAS AN ARROW

Time has an arrow
a quiver in a bow
drawn in pent-up tension
and pointing straight to Now—
All the things we see and hear,
the things we smell and taste—
are knit together to create
this thrilling Pearl of Life.
A sometimes graceful passage we infer
through sense and touch—
Beauty past description.
A Gift beyond all price.

The Picture

See-his arm is draped
with ease
across the smooth cold stone
and Oh!
his strong scarred wrist is
offered naked—
freely turning up and outward—
sun streams down his face
and traces
crevices deepened by his smile
(As I would trace with my forefinger
if somehow I were there.)
His hand lies curved
and gently open
as if he just let go of
something
as if he had received a
Blessing
or finally comes in
Peace

The Moon is Known Best

The moon is known best
By the obsessed
Not when full lit
By the sun's fit
Harsh wash
But rather when stunted
Blunted by dark
Waxing or waning
And cut through stark
By the terminus
Her nemesis
Where blue black spills
To fill
craters in relief
So the eye that peers
With new belief
Through atmospheric dust
With a lust
To know her
May come to expect
To see her defects
For the very first time
Revealed through the truth
The proof
Of terminus.

We Walked a Path of Memory

We walked a path of memory
under holy limbs of arching trees—
hands entwined, minds engaged—
we stopped by ponds refracting light
where past loves floated
Ophelia-like,
watery and faint,
among the tainted pads of trailing Lilies.
And we began to exorcise
the ghosts of lovers past—
a great and early test!
(so soon, so brave)
At last—
Our resolute bid for
Acceptance sacred.
We recounted fully
each encounter
each counted joining
or enjoining—
whether casual or fierce-
fair or foul—
healing or toxic.
As we remembered,
we measured
Restraint.
We acknowledged
Abandon.
We abandoned

CANTO CONTINUED

Fear as
we forgave
drips of weakness on
fallen leaves that littered the trail
we deliberately trod.
We Forgave it all
and then went on
to Bless it all
as we must
for each old story
bought us trust,
each taken step towards
Transparency's Cusp—
as light streamed through us,
the lilies of the pond,
and the leaves trembling
in the blue-gold sky.

BOOK-END DEDICATION

So here, at the end of this book, you emerge from your meanderings through the labyrinth of my interior life. I can't tell you how amazed I am that someone chose to join me here.

Thank you for spending your time reading my poems, and if any inspired you to be just a little more conscious of the blessings in your life, then I am grateful beyond the words I used to create them.

Promise me this: you will pass on your love and ability to accept, and comfort a little girl against the wall, or a lost and crying boy—whether that child is in you, or beside you.

Thank you for that.

Patricia Thrushart

June 1, 2009

ABOUT THE AUTHOR

Patricia Thrushart is the pseudonym for a woman 'of middling age' who lives in Western Pennsylvania with her two children. Her eclectic college career led to degrees in Liberal Arts and a Masters in Public Management, and informs her writing far more than her work as a senior executive for one of the businesses pursued by a large money center bank. In keeping with the theme of her college studies, she has a myriad of interests she has pursued, as her little voice often reminds her, to a level of competency but not mastery, including the performance of early music on voice and instruments, martial arts, horseback riding, bird-watching, and domestic pursuits. She lives today in a little town outside a major metropolitan city, but hopes someday to live in the country with her two horses, some chickens and maybe a goat. And lots of books.

www.ingramcontent.com/pod-product-compliance
Lightning Source LLC
LaVergne TN
LVHW051848080426
835512LV00018B/3129